STRENGTH
FOR THE
CLIMB

**30 DAYS OF FAITH, HEALING &
HOPE.**

By

SAMU NDHLOVU

STRENGTH FOR THE CLIMB

www.usapublishinghub.com

Published by: USA Publishing Hub

Printed In United States of America

Table of Contents

BONUS PRAYER

DEDICATION

To everyone climbing their own mountain, may you find strength for every step.

SCRIPTURE

ACKNOWLEDGMENT

Scripture quotations, including Psalm 46:10, are taken from the Holy Bible, New International Version® (NIV). Used by permission. All rights reserved worldwide.

INTRODUCTION

Life is filled with mountains. Some rise quietly from within us, formed by unspoken fears, unresolved pain, unanswered prayers, and seasons of waiting. Others appear without warning through sudden loss, unexpected transitions, broken relationships, health challenges, financial strain, or moments that shift life in ways we never anticipated. There are emotional climbs that stretch our hearts beyond comfort, spiritual climbs that refine and deepen our faith, and physical or practical climbs that test our endurance. Some mountains excite us and awaken purpose, while others exhaust us, breaking us down before they slowly begin to rebuild us. Yet through every climb, every tear, every quiet triumph, and every whispered prayer, God remains present.

Often, we assume that strength must look confident and unshaken. We believe faith should always feel steady and clear. But real strength is often formed in hidden places. It is shaped during silent prayers, private tears, and moments when simply getting through the day feels like an accomplishment. God does not meet us only at the summit. He meets us on the steep paths, the uneven ground, the pauses taken to catch our breath, and the days when the climb feels overwhelming. He walks with us through every step.

This 30 day devotional was born out of a season filled with such mountains. It was shaped in moments of silence when answers did not come, moments of surrender when holding on felt impossible, moments of fear when the future felt uncertain, and moments of unexpected grace when God revealed His faithfulness in quiet yet powerful ways. The reflections within these pages are drawn from real experiences, real struggles, and real encounters with God's presence and strength in the middle of weakness.

There were seasons when progress felt slow and faith felt fragile. Days when hope seemed distant and nights when prayer became the only place of rest. Yet even in those moments, God was working. Sometimes His work was gentle and unseen, but it was always faithful. He did not remove every mountain, but He provided the strength to climb them. He did not rush the process, but He remained constant through it. This devotional reflects that truth. Healing takes time. Growth is gradual. God's presence is steady even when life feels uncertain.

This book is not about perfection. It is about progress. It is not about having all the answers. It is about learning to trust God in the questions. It is not about avoiding hardship. It is about discovering strength in the midst of it. Some days you may feel hopeful and encouraged. Other days you may feel tired, discouraged, or unsure. Both are part of the journey, and both are welcome here.

Over the next thirty days, my prayer is that you encounter the God who meets you in stillness when life grows quiet, the God who strengthens you when the climb feels heavy, and the God who walks beside you when the path ahead feels unclear. I hope you discover the courage to trust Him in uncertainty, the power of prayer in difficult moments, and healing that begins deep within the heart. May you find hope that anchors your soul, peace that steadies your spirit, and the quiet beauty of new beginnings unfolding in God's perfect time.

Each day is designed to meet you where you are. You do not need to rush. You do not need to compare your journey to anyone else's. Whether you read one day at a time or return to certain reflections again and again, allow these pages to be a gentle companion that offers encouragement, scripture, and prayer as you continue your climb.

Whether you stand at the base of the mountain unsure of where to begin, halfway through the climb feeling weary yet determined, or near the summit reflecting on all you have endured, this devotional is for you. My prayer is that you feel God's hand lifting you when you are tired, guiding you when the way feels unclear, and comforting you when the climb feels heavy. You are not forgotten. You are not behind. You are not walking alone.

Your journey matters.

Your climb has purpose.

Your story is still unfolding.

May these pages remind you that God walks with you, strengthens you, and meets you at every stage of the climb. Let us begin this journey together, one day, one prayer, and one step of faith at a time.

With love and faith,

PART I

Days 1–5

Day 1

When God Begins With Silence

Psalm 46:10

"Be still, and know that I am God."

There are moments when heaven feels quiet, when prayers seem unanswered, and when God feels distant. Silence can be unsettling, especially in seasons when life feels heavy and uncertain.

I remember a time when everything seemed to fall apart at once, a failed marriage, major surgery, and financial struggles. In those moments, I felt abandoned, unseen, and overwhelmed. Looking back now, I realize that God's silence was not absence. It was an invitation.

One day, while sitting in a restaurant, a friend gently reminded me to sit in stillness and listen. At first, that felt impossible. My thoughts were loud, my heart was broken, and my fears drowned out everything else.

But it was in stillness that I finally heard God's whispers. Silence became sacred. Stillness became strength. And God's presence, subtle at first, became clearer than I expected.

When life grows quiet, God is not ignoring you. He is preparing you. He is grounding you. He is drawing you closer so you can hear His plan.

Reflection

What area of your life feels silent right now?

How can stillness help you hear God's voice more clearly?

Prayer

Lord, help me embrace Your stillness. Quiet my heart so I can hear Your voice. Remind me that even in silence, You are working and You are near. Amen.

Day 2

Leaning on God

Proverbs 3:5–6

"Trust in the Lord with all your heart and lean not on your own understanding."

Trusting God sounds simple, until life forces you to actually do it.

I remember moving to Canada with big dreams of becoming a nurse. I enrolled in classes, chemistry, statistics, nutrition, and gave everything I had. When I didn't pass some of those classes, I felt ashamed and defeated.

Looking back, what felt like failure was actually redirection. God closed a door I was forcing open and led me toward a career better suited for my gifts, one that became far more fulfilling than anything I had imagined.

Life rarely goes according to our plans, but it always goes according to God's purpose. Trust means letting go of your blueprint and embracing His. It means believing He knows better, even when it hurts. It means surrendering when your plans fall apart, because His plans are better.

Reflection

What failed plan might God be redirecting in your life?

Where is God asking you to lean on Him instead of yourself?

Prayer

Lord, help me trust Your plans even when mine fall apart. Lead me in Your wisdom and remind me that every step with You is purposeful. Amen.

Day 3

The Weight of Waiting

Isaiah 40:31

"But those who wait on the Lord shall renew their strength…"

Waiting is one of the most difficult spiritual disciplines. It stretches you, humbles you, exposes your fears, and tests your faith.

There were seasons when I felt stuck, watching others move forward while I remained in the same place. Just like the dry bones in Ezekiel's vision, I longed to live again. I asked God "How long?" more times than I can remember.

Waiting is not punishment. Waiting is preparation.

It is in waiting that God strengthens our spiritual muscles. It is in waiting that He purifies our motives. It is in waiting that He aligns us with His timing.

You may feel delayed, but you are not denied.

You may feel overlooked, but heaven has not forgotten you.

You may feel stuck, but God is crafting something ahead that you cannot yet see.

Waiting is where strength is built, one quiet moment at a time.

Reflection

What part of your life feels on hold?

How might God be preparing you during this waiting season?

Prayer

Lord, give me strength while I wait. Renew my faith and help me trust that Your timing is perfect. Amen.

Day 4

When Life Feels Too Heavy

Psalm 34:18

"The Lord is close to the brokenhearted…"

There are seasons when life feels suffocating, when the weight of grief, disappointment, or hardship feels too heavy to carry.

I have had moments when even breathing felt difficult, when darkness felt closer than hope. Those were wilderness seasons, dry, exhausting, and uncertain.

The Israelites spent forty years wandering in the wilderness, feeling stuck and forgotten. Yet even there, God sustained them. Even there, He was present.

Life will bring wilderness seasons, but God does not leave you in them alone. He strengthens you in the dryness. He comforts you in the heaviness. He walks with you through the shadows.

Just because your journey feels heavy does not mean God is distant. Often, He is closest in the seasons that feel the hardest.

Reflection

What wilderness season are you walking through?

How has God strengthened you during difficult times?

Prayer

Lord, when life feels too heavy, remind me that You are near. Carry me when I cannot carry myself. Amen.

Day 5

Breaking Point of Faith

---

2 Corinthians 12:9

"My grace is sufficient for you, for My power is made perfect in weakness."

There are moments when people notice your flaws before they recognize your progress, when your mistakes echo louder than your growth.

I have felt judged, misunderstood, and defined by my past. Yet in those breaking-point moments, God's grace became my greatest comfort.

I think of the woman who touched Jesus' garment, rejected, isolated, and labeled unclean. Jesus called her daughter and restored her instantly. I also think of the woman caught in adultery, surrounded by accusers ready to condemn her. Jesus stepped in front of her shame and covered her with mercy.

When the world defines you by your failures, God defines you by His grace. You are not disqualified by your weaknesses. You are positioned for His power to shine through them.

Reflection

Where have you felt judged or misunderstood?

How has God shown you grace in those moments?

Prayer

Lord, thank You for Your grace that meets me in my weakness. Help me see myself the way You see me, redeemed, loved, and restored. Amen.

PART II

Days 6–10

Day 6

The Cry for Help

Psalm 61:2

"From the end of the earth I will cry to You; when my heart is overwhelmed, lead me to the rock that is higher than I."

Have you ever been lost physically, emotionally, or spiritually, wandering without even realizing you have drifted away from safety?

As a young child, I once got lost on a train. While my family searched every car in a panic, I was happily visiting with passengers, unaware that I was even missing. Eventually, they found me. I had not cried for help, yet they came anyway.

This is how God cares for us.

We do not always recognize when we are lost. We do not always realize how far we have wandered. But God sees. God knows. And even before we call, He is already on His way to find us.

When your heart is overwhelmed, God is your Rock

stable, steady, unshaken. He does not wait for you to have everything together. He comes to you in your wandering. He restores you even before you fully understand that you need rescuing.

Reflection

In what areas of your life have you wandered unintentionally?

How has God found you even before you asked?

Prayer

Lord, when I am overwhelmed or lost, lead me back to You. Thank You for pursuing me even when I do not realize I need rescuing. Amen.

Day 7

Beauty in His Time

Ecclesiastes 3:11

"He has made everything beautiful in His time."

A Season of Reflection

There are moments when life slows down just long enough for us to look back and wonder how we made it through certain seasons. These moments often come quietly, sometimes in the middle of an ordinary day, and they surprise us with gratitude or clarity. Today brought one of those moments for me.

I remembered a time when I had only five dollars to my name. Rent was due. Tuition payments were looming. My cupboards were almost empty. I had no insurance, no gas money, and no idea how I would make it through the week, let alone the semester. The weight of fear and uncertainty pressed heavily on me. In that quiet desperation, I questioned God's purpose for my life, and in my darkest thoughts, I even wondered if life itself was worth holding onto.

But just as despair tightened its grip, God stepped in.

When God Steps In

During that painful season, God sent someone into my life, a student advisor who recognized my struggle and offered the compassion I desperately needed. Through her, I received scholarship funds that covered every essential need. What seemed impossible suddenly became possible. What felt like the end became a beginning of God's provision.

Looking back, I can now see that God was working even when I felt nothing. He was moving pieces into place long before I cried out for help. My circumstances did not transform overnight, but hope returned. Strength returned. Possibility returned. And my faith deepened.

A Reminder for Every Season

As I reflect on that season, I am overwhelmed by the countless ways God has shown up for me, especially at the edge of my breaking points. His timing rarely aligned with mine, yet it always proved perfect. What felt like delay was preparation. What felt like silence was positioning. What felt like abandonment was His protection.

God makes all things beautiful in His time, not ours. Your life is no exception. You may not understand the season you are in. You may feel surrounded by questions, fears, or needs. But God's faithfulness does not depend on your circumstances. He is working in ways you cannot yet see.

Reflection Questions

Where in your life do you feel like you are waiting on God's timing?

How has God shown up for you in seasons when all hope felt lost?

What unfinished areas of your life might God be preparing to make beautiful?

A Prayer for Today

Father, thank You for reminding me that Your timing is perfect, even when my circumstances feel overwhelming. Help me trust You in every season, especially the ones that stretch my faith. Remind me of the times You have carried me and provided for me. Make all things beautiful in Your time, and strengthen my heart as I wait. Amen.

Day 8

When Hope Is Barely Holding On

Romans 15:13

"May the God of hope fill you with all joy and peace as you trust in Him…"

Hope is not always loud. Sometimes it flickers, barely bright enough to hold onto.

There are days when hope feels fragile, when the weight of life drains your strength and your prayers feel thin. But the beauty of Romans 15:13 is that hope does not come from you. Hope comes from God.

Even when your hope is weak, His hope is strong. Even when you feel empty, He can fill you to overflowing. One song, one verse, one moment in His presence can reignite the flame.

Your hope does not need to be strong. God is strong enough for both of you.

Reflection

Where does hope feel fragile for you today?

What small reminders has God given you to encourage you?

Prayer

Lord, fill me with Your hope when mine feels weak. Strengthen my faith and remind me that You are the God who restores joy and peace. Amen.

Day 9

God in the Midnight Moments

Acts 16:25–26

"About midnight Paul and Silas were praying and singing hymns to God… and suddenly there was a violent earthquake…"

There are moments when you need God to show up in a way that changes everything, moments when only He can break chains you cannot break yourself.

Paul and Silas praised God at midnight, a time symbolizing darkness, uncertainty, and waiting. Their praise shifted the atmosphere, and God moved.

Today I thought about how my own struggles, especially the moments when I felt at my lowest, unexpectedly became opportunities to bless others. Someone once gifted me a book they had written, thanking me for the encouragement I had given them, even though I was walking through my own midnight season.

God creates miracles in ordinary moments. Your darkest midnight can become someone else's testimony. God uses your pain to shine His light.

Reflection

What midnight moment are you waiting for God to transform?

How has your struggle inspired or strengthened someone else?

Prayer

Lord, thank You for stepping into my midnight moments. Use my life, even in difficult seasons, to shine Your light and impact others. Amen.

Day 10

Even Here, God Is With You

Deuteronomy 31:8

"The Lord Himself goes before you and will be with you…"

At the end of heartbreak, disappointment, loss, or uncertainty, one truth remains: God never leaves.

Even when relationships end, jobs fall through, or plans crumble, God is steady. He walks beside you even when you cannot feel His footsteps.

You may not understand why certain things ended, but God sees the bigger picture. He goes before you into every chapter. Even here, in this moment, in this pain, in this transition, God is with you. And He is already preparing what comes next.

Reflection

Where do you need the reminder that God is with you?

What small signs of His presence have you noticed lately?

Prayer

Lord, thank You for walking with me through every season. Help me trust that You go before me and prepare the way ahead. Amen.

PART III

Days 11–15

Day 11

The God Who Provides

***

Philippians 4:19

"And my God will supply all your needs according to His riches in glory in Christ Jesus."

There is something deeply comforting about remembering how God has provided in the past. Not in small ways, but in ways that prove He sees every need, every tear, and every quiet prayer.

I remember a season when I had no food, my cupboards were empty, and fear was loud. Then God sent people, organizations, and unexpected kindness that filled my table. It was not luck. It was divine provision.

God has provided through a school advisor who went the extra mile, a friend who shared groceries, someone who quietly offered money, and doors that opened at the perfect moment.

God uses people as vessels to meet our needs. He provides like He does for the lilies and the birds, faithfully, abundantly, and sometimes mysteriously.

Thank Him when you have plenty.

Thank Him when you have little.

His provision never fails.

Reflection

What need has God met unexpectedly in your life?

Who has God used to bless you?

Prayer

Lord, thank You for being my Provider. Help me trust Your timing and Your ways, knowing You never fail to meet my needs. Amen.

Day 12

Strength for the Climb

Nehemiah 8:10

"...for the joy of the Lord is your strength."

On a long road trip, you prepare carefully with water, food, fuel, music, and rest stops. Without preparation, the journey becomes much harder than it needs to be.

Life is the same.

We need spiritual provisions for the journey ahead: daily prayer, God's Word, worship, community, and physical nourishment. These strengthen us for the mountains we must climb.

When we are spiritually filled, even stormy paths feel lighter. Hard climbs become manageable. Heavy burdens lose their weight.

With God's joy as your strength, the journey becomes sweeter, and you may even find yourself smiling through the storm.

Reflection

What spiritual fuel do you need more of right now?

How does spending time with God strengthen your journey?

Prayer

Lord, fill me with Your joy. Strengthen me for the climbs ahead and prepare my heart daily through Your Word and Your presence. Amen.

Day 13

Faith Over Fear

Joshua 1:9

"Be strong and courageous… for the Lord your God will be with you wherever you go."

As a child, I was terrified of the dark. Once, while home alone, I turned on every light and played music loudly so I wouldn't hear the noises of the house. I had faith in lights and noise, not in God.

Fear makes us cling to whatever feels safe, but faith calls us to cling to God, especially in the dark.

I think of Shadrach, Meshach, and Abednego facing a blazing furnace. Their courage did not come from confidence in themselves but from confidence in God. They believed He could deliver them, and even if He did not, they would still trust Him.

That is faith over fear. That is courage. That is surrender.

Fear whispers, "You are alone."

Faith declares, "God is here."

Reflection

What fear do you need to surrender today?

How can you choose courage in this season?

Prayer

Lord, give me strength to choose faith over fear. Remind me that You are with me, even in the fire. Amen.

Day 14

The Road That Requires Courage

Psalm 27:1

"The Lord is my light and my salvation, whom shall I fear?"

Some decisions change your life. Some require you to stand alone. Some demand a level of courage you did not know you had.

I have had to make decisions with uncertain outcomes and consequences that were mine alone to face, such as beginning a new job in a remote town. These choices felt overwhelming, but they were necessary.

This reminds me of Esther, who was positioned in the palace for such a time as this. She had to choose between silence or courage, comfort or calling, fear or faith. Her courage saved a nation.

Sometimes God calls you to stand up, speak up, or walk away. Not because it is easy, but because you are chosen for such a time as this.

Reflection

What decision is requiring courage from you right now?

How does Esther's story encourage you?

Prayer

Lord, give me courage for the road ahead. Strengthen me to stand boldly in the purpose You have for me. Amen.

Day 15

The Journey Toward Purpose

Ephesians 2:10

"For we are His workmanship… created for good works…"

In high school, students with the highest grades were invited to stand at the front during chapel. It was an honor that made everyone strive to excel.

We all long to be called out, chosen, and recognized. But God does not choose us based on performance. He chooses us based on identity.

You are His workmanship, His masterpiece, crafted with intention and purpose.

Being chosen means you are set apart, valued, and created with divine intention. There is no qualification required. God chooses you even when you are hurt, broken, discouraged, or lost.

Your purpose is not earned.

It is given.

Reflection

What part of your identity do you struggle to accept?

How does knowing you are God's workmanship strengthen you?

Prayer

Lord, thank You for choosing me. Help me walk confidently in the purpose You designed for me. Amen.

PART IV

Days 16–20

Day 16

Anchored in Hope

Hebrews 6:19

"We have this hope as an anchor for the soul, firm and secure."

Hope is gentle, yet powerful. It steadies you. It lifts you. It anchors your soul in seasons when everything feels uncertain.

Today I thought of farmers and how they plant seeds with hope that rain will come and a harvest will follow. They work, they wait, and they trust.

I reflected on the small things that give me hope: a song that arrives at the perfect moment, a scripture that breathes life into my spirit, and the quiet assurance that things will get better.

I also remembered Job, a man who lost everything yet refused to let go of hope. In unimaginable pain, he declared, "Though He slay me, yet will I hope in Him."

Hope does not deny pain. Hope anchors you through it. Even when life trembles, your soul does not have to.

Reflection

What anchors your hope when life feels shaky?

What small gifts of hope has God given you lately?

Prayer

Lord, anchor my soul in Your promises. Fill me with hope that is steady, strong, and secure. Amen.

Day 17

Becoming a Witness

Revelation 12:11

"They overcame… by the word of their testimony."

Your story has power. Your testimony can change lives.

I thought about the healed blind man who ran to tell everyone what Jesus had done for him. He did not need perfect words or a polished message. His transformation spoke for itself.

When God touches your life, staying silent becomes impossible. Healed people speak. Restored people testify. Those who have seen God move cannot keep quiet.

Your testimony is someone else's hope. Your victory is someone else's encouragement. Your story is someone else's roadmap to faith.

Let your life shine. Share what God has done.

Reflection

What part of your testimony is God asking you to share?

Who in your life needs encouragement from your story?

Prayer

Lord, thank You for the testimony You have given me. Help me share it boldly and humbly for Your glory. Amen.

Day 18

Faithfulness in the Small Things

Luke 16:10

"Whoever is faithful with little will also be faithful with much…"

Faithfulness often appears in the smallest moments, not in grand gestures but in quiet obedience.

Today I reflected on the widow of Zarephath. She had almost nothing, just enough flour and oil for one last meal. Yet God asked her to give from the little she had. She obeyed in faith, and God multiplied what she offered.

Sometimes we are paralyzed by fear, scarcity, or worry. Sometimes obedience makes no sense to those around us. But God sees every small act of trust.

Little in God's hands becomes more than enough.

Reflection

Where is God asking you to be faithful with a little?

What small act of obedience can you offer today?

Prayer

Lord, help me be faithful in the little things. Teach me to trust You even when my resources feel small. Amen.

Day 19

The Mountains Within

Mark 11:23

"If anyone says to this mountain, 'Be removed'… it will be done."

Sometimes the mountains we face are not external but internal. Fear, doubt, shame, worry, trauma, and insecurity can rise within us and feel impossible to overcome.

There have been moments when I needed God to do the impossible, and He did. Just as He helped Joshua when he prayed for the sun to stand still and strengthened Samson when all strength had left him, God strengthens us for the mountains inside us.

God often shakes us within before shifting anything around us. Your internal mountains are no match for His power. He strengthens you to move what once felt immovable.

Reflection

What internal mountain do you need God to help you move today?

How have past struggles strengthened your faith?

Prayer

Lord, strengthen me from within and give me faith to speak to the mountains in my life. Amen.

Day 20

Choosing Trust Over Control

Psalm 37:5

"Commit your way to the Lord; trust in Him, and He will act."

Trying to control what God is asking us to surrender will always lead to chaos rather than peace.

I have held onto relationships, plans, and dreams that I knew were not right, driven by fear, loneliness, or the need to have things my way. But control never leads to clarity. Control leads to exhaustion.

Today I thought about Jonah, who ran from God because he did not agree with His plan. Jonah took control, and it led him into a storm, a shipwreck, and the belly of a whale. When he finally surrendered, God redirected him.

Trust means letting go.

Trust means releasing outcomes.

Trust means believing God knows what you cannot see.

Let go, and let God lead.

Reflection

What are you trying to control instead of surrendering to God?

What would trusting God look like for you today?

Prayer

Lord, I release what I have been trying to control. Lead me, guide me, and help me trust Your way above my own. Amen.

PART V

Days 21–25

Day 21

Walking in Freedom

John 8:36

"So if the Son sets you free, you will be free indeed."

Freedom does not always arrive with fireworks. Sometimes it enters quietly, through moments of relief, clarity, or peace.

Today I reflected on the moment my divorce judgment came through. It marked the end of a painful chapter, but it also marked the beginning of freedom. I felt God lifting a weight I had carried far too long.

It reminded me of Paul and Silas, whose chains fell off while they worshiped in prison. Their freedom came suddenly, unexpectedly, and miraculously.

Freedom begins the moment you surrender. The moment you release what is breaking you. The moment you choose God over fear.

To walk in freedom means declaring victory even before you see it, trusting God even when your heart trembles, choosing peace where there once was chaos, standing firm in your identity, and recognizing that your past no longer has power over you.

You are free, not because of your strength, but because of Christ.

Reflection

What chains has God recently broken in your life?

Where do you need to embrace freedom more fully?

Prayer

Lord, thank You for the freedom You have given me. Help me walk boldly in it each day. Amen.

Day 22

When God Restores What Was Lost

Joel 2:25

"I will restore to you the years that the locust has eaten…"

Restoration is rarely instant. It comes step by step, little by little, grace by grace.

I reflected today on how God restores us. Your smile begins to return. Your sleep becomes peaceful again. Fear fades. Confidence grows. Finances stabilize. Joy brightens. Purpose becomes clearer.

God rebuilt Ruth's life from the ashes of heartbreak and loss. She did not know that Boaz, or a future filled with love and purpose, was waiting on the other side of her obedience and faithfulness.

The prodigal son experienced restoration as well. His father ran to embrace him, with a robe, a ring, and a celebration prepared.

God restores gently, thoroughly, lovingly, and in His perfect time.

What you lost is not the end of your story. It is the beginning of God's rebuilding.

Reflection

Where do you see signs of God restoring you?

What area of your life do you need to trust Him with?

Prayer

Lord, thank You for restoring my strength, joy, and purpose. Continue rebuilding what was broken and renewing what was lost. Amen.

Day 23

Healing From the Inside Out

Psalm 147:3

"He heals the brokenhearted and binds up their wounds."

Healing is not always visible. Sometimes the deepest wounds are the ones hidden inside.

I thought about the paralyzed man at Bethesda. He was unable to move and stuck in the same place for years, waiting for someone to help him. Jesus did not only heal his body. He restored his identity, dignity, and hope.

Many of us are paralyzed in different ways: pride, grudges, anxiety, unforgiveness, anger, depression, or fear. We may be walking physically, but spiritually stuck.

True healing begins inside, in the places we avoid, in the wounds we hide, and in the emotions we suppress.

When God heals the inside, the outside begins to change. Your interactions soften. Your perspective shifts. Your relationships mend. Your spirit begins to shine again.

Healing is a journey, one God walks with you step by step.

Reflection

What area of your heart needs inner healing today?

What internal paralysis has kept you stuck?

Prayer

Lord, heal me from the inside out. Restore every part of me that has been wounded, hidden, or broken. Make me whole in You. Amen.

Day 24

Renewing Your Mind

Romans 12:2

"Be transformed by the renewing of your mind…"

There are times when the pressure to fit in feels overwhelming, when pleasing others becomes easier than standing for truth.

I thought of Ananias and Sapphira, who wanted to look good before people but lied to God instead. Their story reminds us that renewing the mind requires honesty, deep, vulnerable honesty before God.

Renewing your mind means confronting the lies you have believed, rejecting worldly pressure, embracing God's truth, and allowing Him to reshape your thoughts.

Transformation begins with truth. Growth begins with surrender. Clarity begins with honesty.

When your mind is renewed, everything else begins to change, your decisions, habits, relationships, priorities, and peace.

Reflection

What lie have you been believing about yourself?

Where do you need God's truth to reshape your thinking?

Prayer

Lord, renew my mind with Your truth. Help me walk in honesty and transformation. Align my thoughts with Your Word. Amen.

Day 25

Stepping Out of Survival Mode

Isaiah 43:19

"See, I am doing a new thing… Do you not perceive it?"

Survival mode often feels necessary, especially when life has been unpredictable. But it can become a prison, keeping you living small, cautious, and fearful.

I reflected today on times when I stretched the little I had, food, energy, resources, just to get through another day. It reminded me of the Israelites and the manna. God provided daily, but not for hoarding. He wanted trust, not fear.

Survival mode blinds you to the new things God is doing. It keeps you guarded when God wants you open. It keeps you cautious when God wants you courageous.

God is calling you out of survival and into abundance. Out of fear and into trust. Out of the old and into the new.

Let go. Open your hands. Step into the new beginning God is preparing.

Reflection

What is keeping you stuck in survival mode?

What new thing is God beginning in your life?

Prayer

Lord, help me step out of survival and into Your abundance. Open my eyes to the new things You are doing. Amen.

PART VI

Days 26–30

Day 26

Becoming Who God Says You Are

1 Peter 2:9

"But you are a chosen people, a royal priesthood... God's special possession."

In high school, students with the highest grades were invited to stand at the front during chapel. It was an honor, one that brought pride to those who were called. Everyone worked hard, hoping their name would be spoken.

We all long to be chosen.

But God's choosing is different. He does not choose based on performance. He does not call you because you are perfect. He calls you because you are His.

To be chosen means that God sees value in you beyond what others see. It means your past cannot disqualify you. It means He has a purpose that only you can fulfill.

To be set apart means God has placed His mark on your life. It means you carry a divine identity. It means you are called to shine in ways the world cannot imitate.

There is no qualification required. God chooses the broken, the discouraged, the overlooked, and the uncertain. Through His grace, He makes them whole, strong, and purposeful.

You are chosen.

You are set apart.

You are God's own.

Reflection

What false labels do you need to release today?

How can you walk confidently in your identity as chosen?

Prayer

Lord, thank You for calling me chosen. Help me see myself through Your eyes and walk boldly in the purpose You created for me. Amen.

Day 27

Protected by His Presence

Psalm 91:1–2

"Whoever dwells in the shelter of the Most High will rest in the shadow of the Almighty…"

There is a unique kind of safety found only in God's presence, a protection that shields, strengthens, and surrounds you.

I thought about Daniel in the lions' den. God did not keep Daniel out of the den. He entered the den with him and shut the lions' mouths.

God's protection does not always mean avoiding hardship. Sometimes it means being covered in the middle of it.

I also reflected on how birds build their nests: secure, hidden, and carefully designed to protect their eggs from danger. The eggs are not strong enough to defend themselves, yet the nest shields them completely.

God's presence is your nest. Your covering. Your shield.

He protects you from threats you never saw coming. He guards you from attacks you did not recognize. He stands between you and danger.

Rest in His shadow. You are safe in His hands.

Reflection

How has God protected you, whether seen or unseen?

Where do you need to trust His covering more deeply?

Prayer

Lord, thank You for Your constant protection. Help me dwell in Your presence and trust that I am safe under Your wings. Amen.

Day 28

Your Life Is a Testimony

~⌒⌒~

Matthew 5:16

"Let your light shine before others…"

When God heals you, restores you, or rescues you, silence becomes impossible.

I think of the man with leprosy who was healed by Jesus. His life changed in an instant, and he could not contain his joy. He told everyone what God had done for him.

Your story carries power. Your testimony carries light. Your breakthrough carries purpose.

You never know who might find hope through what God has done in your life. Your story may be the confirmation someone is praying for. Your healing may be the encouragement someone else needs.

Let your life shine.

Tell your story boldly.

Live as a testimony of God's grace.

Reflection

What testimony do you need to share more openly?

Who could be blessed by hearing what God has done for you?

Prayer

Lord, thank You for the miracles and healing You bring. Help me share my testimony with boldness and humility. Amen.

Day 29

God of the Unexpected

Genesis 32:26–28

"…I will not let You go unless You bless me."

God often works through the unexpected, through situations that stretch us, struggles that push us, and moments that make us wrestle with ourselves and with Him.

Jacob wrestled with God all night. He wrestled with fear, identity, and his past. Because he held on, God blessed him and renamed him Israel.

Sometimes God allows us to wrestle because something new is being birthed.

I also think of Balaam's donkey, when God opened its mouth to speak. An unexpected moment that saved Balaam's life.

God uses unusual situations to redirect you, awaken you, or protect you. The unexpected is often the place where God's greatest miracles begin.

May God surprise you.

May He speak to you in unexpected ways.

May He bless you after every battle.

Reflection

What are you wrestling with today?

How might God be working through the unexpected?

Prayer

Lord, help me hold onto You during the wrestle. Bless me after the battle and open my eyes to Your unexpected miracles. Amen.

Day 30

The Journey Continues

2 Corinthians 5:17

"The old has gone, the new is here!"

Every ending is also a beginning. Every chapter that closes makes room for a new story written by God's hand.

Today I reflected on the beauty of new beginnings. They bring new paths, new goals, new vision, new strength, and new courage.

Just as Noah stepped out of the ark into a world washed clean, new beginnings often follow seasons of storms. Noah did not step into just a new land. He stepped into new purpose, new hope, new responsibility, new grace, and new life.

As you enter your next chapter, remember to put on the full armor of God. Not because the journey will be easy, but because you are equipped.

Give thanks in every season.

Reflect on how far God has brought you.

Recognize the beauty of the new He is forming.

Your journey does not end here. It continues, with God leading the way.

Reflection

What new beginning is God leading you into?

What do you need to leave behind from the old season?

Prayer

Lord, thank You for new beginnings. Strengthen me for the journey ahead and help me walk confidently into the future You have prepared. Amen.

CONCLUSION

The Climb Was Worth It

You have made it through thirty days of reflection, healing, faith, and renewal. But this is not the end. It is the beginning of a stronger, more courageous, and more spiritually grounded version of you.

Every mountain you climbed prepared you for the next.

Every prayer strengthened your soul.

Every scripture shaped your heart.

Every breakthrough deepened your faith.

You are not who you used to be. God has done a new work in you, and the journey continues with fresh vision, restored hope, and renewed strength.

Wherever life leads next, remember this: God climbs with you.

Step by step.

Breath by breath.

Day by day.

You are stronger now.

You are more grounded now.

You are more hopeful now.

And the best is still ahead.

FINAL BLESSING

May God go before you and prepare every path.

May His presence cover you like a shield.

May His peace surround you in every season.

May His joy strengthen you for every climb.

May His love heal every hidden place.

May His hope anchor you in every storm.

May His favor rest upon your life,

and may your story continue to shine as a testimony of His goodness.

You are loved.

You are chosen.

You are strengthened.

You are never alone.

Amen.

BONUS PRAYER

Strength for the Climb

———— ❧ ❦ ————

Heavenly Father,

You see the mountain before me and the path beneath my feet. You know the weight I carry, the fears I wrestle with, and the strength it takes just to keep moving forward. Today, I place every step of this journey into Your hands.

When the climb feels steep and my strength feels small, remind me that I do not climb alone. Be my source of endurance when I feel tired, my courage when fear rises, and my peace when the road feels uncertain. Help me trust You not only at the summit, but in every moment along the way.

Teach me to release what is holding me back and to carry only what You have given me. Replace my doubt with faith, my worry with hope, and my weariness with renewed strength. When progress feels slow, help me see that You are still working—even in the quiet, unseen places.

Thank You for walking with me through every valley and up every mountain. Thank You for shaping me through the climb and preparing me for what lies ahead. I trust You with the journey, the timing, and the outcome.

I will keep going—not because I am strong on my own, but because You are with me, strengthening me step by step.

Amen.

ABOUT THE AUTHOR

Samu Ndhlovu is a counsellor, writer, and speaker with a deep calling to help women heal emotionally, grow spiritually, and rediscover the strength God has placed within them. Through her counselling work, writing, and ministry, she creates safe and compassionate spaces where women feel seen, heard, and supported as they navigate life's most challenging seasons. Her approach gently weaves professional insight with faith, allowing meaningful and lasting healing to take place at both the heart and soul level.

Having walked through her own valleys marked by silence, loss, rebuilding, and renewal, Samu brings authenticity and empathy to everything she does. She understands the complexity of emotional pain and the courage it takes to face it honestly. Her words are shaped by both lived experience and her counselling practice, reflecting a God who meets His children in moments of weakness and patiently walks with them toward restoration. She believes healing is a journey that unfolds step by step, faith is a daily choice, and every climb, no matter how difficult carries purpose when God is present.

Strength for the Climb was born from Samu's personal journey through life's mountains and the quiet, often unseen ways God revealed His faithfulness along the way. This book reflects her counsellor's heart, to encourage women to keep going, to trust the process of healing, and to find strength in God even when the path feels uncertain. It serves as both a gentle companion and a source of spiritual grounding for women seeking hope, clarity, and renewal in their lives.

Samu is deeply committed to walking alongside women who feel weary, overwhelmed, or unsure of their next step. She recognizes that healing does not follow a straight path and that growth often requires patience, reflection, and intentional surrender. Through her work, she invites women to extend grace to themselves, to face difficult emotions with honesty, and to remain open to God's guidance throughout the journey.

Beyond her professional work, Samu values stillness, intentional living, and moments of quiet reflection that allow space for spiritual renewal. She finds joy in quiet mornings, worship music, nature walks, reflective journaling, and meaningful conversations that uplift, heal, and inspire the soul. Her life and work are grounded in a simple yet enduring truth: God's strength is always sufficient, healing is possible, and no woman is ever meant to walk her journey alone. Each step forward, taken in faith matters.